Let's Play Tag!

📖 Read the Page

▶ Read the Story

⭐ Game

😊 Yes   ☹ No

🔁 Repeat

⬛ Stop

ni hao, kai-lan

Kai-lan's Super Sleepover

written by Amy Keating Rogers

illustrated by Warner McGee

original telescreenplay by May Chan

1

"Ni hao! I'm Kai-lan," says Kai-lan. "Ni hao is how I say 'hi' in Chinese. Tonight I'm having a super special sleepover with all my friends! Will you come too?"

Outside, Kai-lan's grandpa, YeYe, sets up a big ladybug tent where everyone will sleep.

Kai-lan's friends Rintoo the tiger and Hoho the monkey arrive for the sleepover.

"Ni men hao," says Kai-lan.

"Ni hao, Kai-lan!" says Rintoo.

"Ni hao!" says Hoho.

"I looooove campouts!" says Rintoo.

But who is this giant panda?

"It's Tolee!" says Kai-lan. "And he's wearing a panda backpack! Tolee loves pandas!"

"Especially my stuffed panda, Pandy!" says Tolee.

"Come on, let's go inside the tent and unpack," says Kai-lan.

The fireflies fly into the lanterns to light up the tent.

"Let's set up our sleeping bags!" says Kai-lan.

"Let's put on our slippers," says Kai-lan.

"Uh oh!" says Hoho. "I can't find mine!"

The tent is such a mess, nobody can find their slippers!

"Let's look for our slippers!" says Kai-lan.

All the friends look and find all the slippers.

"Let's play Flashlight Funny Faces!"
says Kai-lan.

"I loooove Flashlight Funny Faces.
Um, how do you play?" asks Rintoo.

"You just hold the flashlight and …
you make a funny face!" says Kai-lan.

"But there's only one flashlight. How
can we all play?" asks Rintoo.

"I'll share my flashlight so everyone
can have a turn!" says Kai-lan.

When everyone finishes making funny
faces they are ready to play something else.

"Hey, Tolee," says Rintoo. "I want to play with Pandy!"

"Me too! Me too!" says Hoho.

"NO! I'm the only one who can play with Pandy!" shouts Tolee.

Tolee leaves the tent with Pandy.

"We gotta, gotta try to find the reason why Tolee left with Pandy!" says Kai-lan.

"Tolee, did you take Pandy away because you didn't want to share him?" asks Kai-lan.

"Yes," says Tolee, "Pandy is mine, and if I share him then I can't play with him."

"It's okay, Tolee," says Kai-lan. "It's really hard to share sometimes."

"I brought my Chinese drum to share so everyone can play with it!" says YeYe.

"Look, Tolee! Everyone is having a good time because everyone gets to play. YeYe gets a turn to play too!" says Kai-lan.

"I GOT IT!"

says Tolee, excited.

"Everyone gets to play when you take turns and share, share, share!"

"Hey, I want everyone to play with Pandy! Let's play Pass the Panda!" says Tolee.

"I looooove Pass the Panda! What's Pass the Panda?" asks Rintoo.

"I pass Pandy to you and you do a silly dance. Then you pass Pandy and SHARE him," says Tolee.

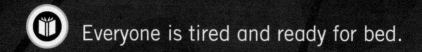
Everyone is tired and ready for bed.

"I'm so glad you came to my super sleepover," says Kai-lan. "Everyone played and everyone shared. You make my heart feel super happy! *Zai jian!*"

The End.

drum

microphone

pipa

tambourine

turntables

xylophone

Super Sleepover Songs

Kai-lan's Clean Up